**Henrietta Lily**

Rosen
REAL
READERS

Rosen
Classroom™
New York

1

Have you ever seen a dam like this? A beaver built this dam. The dam stops a stream from flowing. It makes a pool of water. Beavers make their homes in the pool.

2

People build dams, too.

Dams change the flow of rivers.

The dams that people make are bigger

than the dams that beavers make.

These are engineers. They make things that solve problems. The problems they solve make life better for us.

Engineers make a plan for a dam. They choose the best place to build the dam. This land is being used for a new dam.

Engineers use many large machines to build a dam. Engineers must choose the right materials for the dam. They make a plan for how the dam will work best.

Engineers have a lot to think about. They must think about how much water the dam must hold back. They must think about what will happen to the river.

The pool a dam makes is called a **reservoir**. Reservoirs are useful. The water can be used for **crops** and for drinking.

Some dams have gates. The gates can
be opened or closed. Engineers decide
how much water should flow through
the gates.

Engineers use dams to create **electricity**. Water is used to create power with special machines. These machines are **generators**.

Engineers build many kinds of dams. They think about the use. They think about the land. They use this information to build the right dam.

# Glossary

**crops** Plants that are grown for food, such as peas, corn, or wheat.

**electricity** Energy we use to power things, such as lights, machines, and appliances.

**generator** A machine that turns one kind of energy into another.

**reservoir** A large natural or man-made pool where water collects.